PRAYERS
That Avail Much
for Children

by
Angela Brown

A Little Castle Book

the Little Castle

Harrison House

Prayers That Avail Much For Children
ISBN 0-89274-296-8

Published by Harrison House, Inc.
P. O. Box 35035
Tulsa, Oklahoma 74153

Printed in the United States of America.

Dedication

This book is dedicated to my children,
Hillarie and Jessica,
who are a constant blessing to their parents
and are abundantly growing in the grace and knowledge
of our Lord Jesus Christ.

—Angela Brown

Dear Friend,

Jesus tells us in Matthew 18:1-6 and 19:13-15 that children are very important to God. God has given you a special ability, called faith, to believe and trust in Him. He wants you to learn to use that faith in prayer.

The prayers in this book are made up of passages from God's Word, the Bible. Before you pray a prayer, it would be helpful for you to look up the verses listed below it and read them aloud. You may want to ask your parents or another adult to help you find them in the Bible. Ask God to help you understand what they mean.

As you pray these prayers aloud, you are actually speaking God's own words. God, our Father, promises us in 1 John 5:14,15 that ***if we ask any thing according to his will, he heareth us: and if we know that he hear us, whatsoever we ask, we know that we have the petitions that we desired of him.*** *In Jeremiah 1:12, God promises us that He will watch over His Word to perform it. As you pray God's Word, He will do it for you!*

It is important that you read and pray God's Word daily. His Holy Spirit will teach you many exciting things about God and about yourself as you think upon His Word day and night. (Joshua 1:8.) Remember: God, your Father, is faithful to His Word!

May you grow abundantly in the grace and knowledge of our Lord Jesus Christ.

—Angela Brown

Dear Parents,

God has given parents a great privilege: that of teaching and training children for the Kingdom of God.

Teaching your child how to pray effectively will help him establish an intimate relationship with God, our Father. Prayer is communication with God, and it is imperative if your child is to know God. A child must understand the order of authority (God, parents, child); and even though he can approach God directly for himself, he must do so according to Scriptural principles. (1 John 5:14,15.)

When a child (no matter how young) confesses Jesus as Lord and believes in his heart that God raised Him from the dead, he is born again and alive unto God. Therefore, he can receive spiritual instruction and act on it with your guidance. Because of a lack of knowledge, many children have developed a misconception of who God is and what He does.

Taking time to teach and train your child about how to pray will establish a closer parent/child relationship. It will provide the opportunity you need to minister to his needs—giving reproof, correcting error, disciplining in obedience, and training in righteousness—equipping your child for every good work. (2 Timothy 3:16,17.)

God is not a ''magician'' or ''genie'' who fulfills whims and fantasies. He is a Father Who desires fellowship. If a child can learn the secret of fellowshipping with God, our Father, in the name of Jesus—aware that the Holy Spirit is his constant Companion, Guide, and Teacher—he will grow up bearing fruit in every good work.

Parents, this book is written as a tool for instruction as you rear your children tenderly in the training, discipline, counsel, and admonition of the Lord.

—Germaine Copeland

President,
Word Ministries, Inc.
Atlanta, Georgia

CONTENTS

Bedtime	13
Choosing Friends	14
Fear	15
Feeling Sad or Lonely	16
Finding Favor with Others	17
Forgiveness	18
Healing Prayer	19
Morning Prayer	20
Sharing and Giving	21
Receiving Salvation	22
Receiving the Holy Spirit	23
Worry	24
My Parents	25
My School	26
Our Country	27
Salvation for Others	28
The Church	29
Prayers of Praise	30

PRAYERS
That Avail Much
for Children

BEDTIME

Father, I sing for joy upon my bed.
I lie down and sleep quietly.
I'm not afraid because You, Lord,
watch over me and keep me safe.
My sleep will be sweet,
and You will bless me.
In Jesus' name, I pray.
Amen.

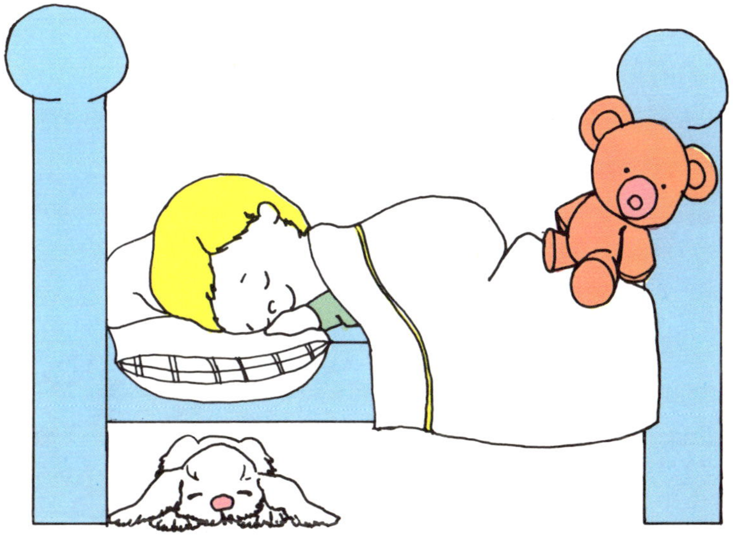

Psalm 149:5
Psalm 4:8
Proverbs 3:24
Psalm 127:2

CHOOSING FRIENDS

Father, I will search for children who please and care about You. I will live in respect and love towards You. I will team up with believers in You, but walk in love toward all people. I will walk with wise friends who know You, and I will be wise.

I will not shame my family, but will obey the laws of God and man. I will keep away from every kind of evil. I roll the work of choosing friends over onto You, and I believe You will cause my thoughts to become agreeable to Your will. Thank You, Father, for watching over Your Word to perform it . . .

in Jesus' name!

2 Corinthians 6:14
Proverbs 13:20
Proverbs 28:7
1 Thessalonians 5:22
Proverbs 16:3 AMP
Jeremiah 1:12 AMP

FEAR

The Lord is my helper.
I will not fear.
The Lord is on my side.
I lean on and trust in Him
completely.
He will keep me from every evil thing,
and under His wings I will be safe.
His truth and faithfulness shield me,
and His angels defend and protect me
when I obey Him.
I'm a disciple, taught of the Lord. I'm calm
and have great peace.
God says, "I will never fail you or leave you
without help. I will not, I will not, I will not
in any way let go of you!"
Thank You, Jesus, for the Holy Spirit Who
lives within me and gives me super-strength
and power to walk unafraid.

Hebrews 13:6
Psalm 118:6
Psalm 91:2,4
Psalm 91:11
Isaiah 54:13 AMP
Hebrews 13:5 AMP
Ephesians 3:16

FEELING SAD OR LONELY

Father, You are my shelter and my protection in times of trouble. I lean on and confidently put my trust in You, because nothing is able to separate me from Your love.

I resist fear, depression, and self-pity. I give the devil no place in me.

Father, I thank You that You lift up those who are sad. Your Word has revived me and given me life. Thank You for giving me a spirit of power, of love, and of a calm and well-balanced mind and discipline and self-control.

I praise You that the joy of the Lord is my strength and stronghold.

Hallelujah!

*Also, read aloud the **Prayers of Praise** (pages 30 and 31).*

Psalm 9:9,10 AMP
Romans 8:38,39
James 4:7
Ephesians 4:27
Psalm 146:8 AMP
Psalm 119:50 AMP
2 Timothy 1:7 AMP
Nehemiah 8:10

FINDING FAVOR WITH OTHERS

Father, in the name of Jesus, You make Your face to shine with joy on me, and You are kind and protective to me. I'm the head and not the tail; I'm above and not beneath. I will try to live as Jesus taught, knowing that You will surround me with pleasure and favor. I will give love and favor to my friends, teachers, parents, etc. (name them) and will be a blessing to them. Thank You, Father, that like Jesus I'm growing strong in spirit, filled with wisdom and favor with God and man.

Numbers 6:25
Deuteronomy 28:13
Psalm 5:12 AMP
Luke 6:38
Luke 2:40
Luke 2:52

FORGIVENESS

Father, in Jesus' name, I will live in peace and love with my family, friends, neighbors, and all the people I meet. I let go of all kinds of meanness, bad temper, anger, and unkindness. With Jesus' help, I will not let the devil use me in any way. And I will treat others the way I want them to treat me. Now, Father, I ask Your forgiveness. I'm sure that You forgive me, because Your Word says You will. And You will forget all my sins. I ask You to forgive all those who have hurt me in any way. And I will forgive them as You do and will forget their wrongdoing also.

Romans 12:10,16-18
Ephesians 4:27,31,32
Luke 6:31
1 John 1:9
Mark 11:25

HEALING PRAYER

Father, I thank You that You are the Lord that heals me. When Jesus walked the earth, He always healed everyone who came to Him. He said He came to earth to do the works of His Father in heaven. I thank You that Jesus died on the cross for my sicknesses as well as my sins. He set me free from *all* sickness of any kind. Now I say with my mouth and believe in my heart that I am healed, in the name of Jesus. Thank You for being a kind and loving Father and for sending me the good gift of healing!

Exodus 15:26
Acts 10:38
John 6:38
1 Peter 2:24
Matthew 8:16,17
Galatians 3:13 (Deuteronomy 28)
Mark 11:23,24
James 1:17

You will build your faith by reading in the Gospels how Jesus healed people.

MORNING PRAYER

Father,
thank You for
keeping me safe
as I slept and for giv-
ing me a new day to enjoy!
I will rejoice and be glad in it!
I trust You with all my works today,
and I know You will make my plans suc-
ceed. Thank You for sending Your angels
with me to protect and keep me as I do the
things You want me to do. I am a disciple, taught
of the Lord, and I will be peaceful and calm all day,
because You, Lord, give me safety and ease me!

It is good to start your day praising the Lord with the ***Prayers of Praise*** *(pages 30 and 31).*

Psalm 118:24
Proverbs 16:3 AMP
Psalm 91:11
Isaiah 54:13
Isaiah 49:25 AMP

SHARING AND GIVING

Father, I thank You that You have blessed me with many wonderful things. I have all that I need out of Your riches in heaven. Your Word says that You have given much to me, so that I can share with many others. And I should give what I have to those in need. I will give to the poor, and You will repay me that which I have given away. I will treat others as I want them to treat me. And I will share all that I have with others, so that the love of Jesus will shine through me!

Philippians 4:19
Deuteronomy 28:12
Luke 6:30
Proverbs 19:17
Luke 6:31
Philippians 2:15

RECEIVING SALVATION*

Father, Your Word says You loved me so much that You sent Your very own Son, Jesus, to die for my sin so I could live with You forever. Jesus said He would give me a new life that is wonderful and rich. I know that I'm a sinner, so I say now that I believe Jesus died for my sin and that You raised Him from the dead.

I thank You for forgetting my sin and for giving me a brand new life. Thank You also for sending the Holy Spirit to teach me and give me power to be like Jesus.

**Read and understand these Scriptures before you pray this prayer:*

John 3:16
John 10:10
Romans 3:23
Romans 10:9,10
2 Corinthians 5:17
John 14:26
John 6:37
2 Corinthians 5:19
John 16:8,9
Romans 5:8
John 14:6
Romans 10:13
John 1:12
2 Corinthians 5:21

RECEIVING THE HOLY SPIRIT

Father, I'm Your child because I have believed in my heart that Jesus took away my sin and that You raised Him from the dead. And I have asked Him to be my Savior.* Jesus said He would ask You to send another Comforter, the Holy Spirit, to teach me all things and to give me power to tell others about the love of Jesus. He also said You would give the Holy Spirit to them that ask. So I ask You now, in Jesus' name, to fill me with Your Holy Spirit. I thank You that I receive Him now. I believe that now I will speak in a new language as the Holy Spirit teaches me new words, so that I may pray to You in secret truths and about hidden things. I thank You that now I have all that I need to be like Jesus!

*See ***Prayer For Receiving Salvation,*** *page 22.*

John 14:16,17,26
Acts 1:8a
Luke 11:13
Acts 2:4
Acts 2:32,33,39
Acts 8:12-17
Acts 10:44-46
Acts 19:2,5,6
1 Corinthians 14:2-15
Ephesians 6:18
Jude 1:20

WORRY

Father, Your Word says that I should not depend on myself, but trust You to help me do all things. So I give You all my cares and worries about ____________________. I believe that You will cause me to have Your thoughts, that I will do the things which please You, and that I will succeed in all that I do. Because Jesus lives in my heart, I have the mind of Christ and hold the thoughts of His heart. I will think only on those things that are good and pure and right and worth praising. I don't have a care. I have the peace that passes all my understanding. Thank You, Jesus!

Proverbs 3:5
1 Peter 5:6,7
Proverbs 16:3 AMP
1 Corinthians 2:16
Philippians 4:8
Philippians 4:6,7

MY PARENTS

I am a disciple, taught of the Lord. I obey my parents as the Lord has taught me, so that I might be well and live long on the earth. My father does not irritate or make me angry; but he treats me tenderly. He trains and disciplines me as the Lord would have him to. I rise up and call my mother blessed. I make my father glad and my mother happy.

My parents will train me up in the way I should go. When I grow older, I will never leave their teaching. Lovingkindness and mercy, truth and faithfulness, will protect them. I thank You, Jesus, for my parents!

Isaiah 54:13 AMP
Ephesians 6:1-4
Proverbs 31:28

Proverbs 10:1
Proverbs 22:6
Proverbs 20:28 AMP

MY SCHOOL

Father, I pray for (name of school) and I thank You for it.

I pray for the teachers and those in places of authority in our school. I believe that skillful and godly wisdom has entered into their hearts and that Your knowledge is pleasant to them. I thank You for born-again, Spirit-filled people to be in authority in our school.

I pray for the students, and I speak Your Word boldly, Father, that we and our households are saved, in the name of Jesus. We will obey You and turn away from whatever might displease You. We will show ourselves to be blameless and innocent children of God in a dark and crooked world, that we will shine out among them like beacon lights, holding out to them the Word of Life.

I praise You, Father, that I see (name of school) walking in the ways of God and honoring Your name. Those who sin will come to the truth, and those who complain will be willing to be taught. Thank You for watching over Your Word to perform it!

Isaiah 29:23,24
Jeremiah 1:12 AMP
Proverbs 2:10 AMP
Acts 16:31
Philippians 2:12,15 AMP

OUR COUNTRY

Father, in Jesus' name, I give thanks for our country and its government. I pray for all the men and women in authority throughout our land. Your Word says that the heart of the king is in the hand of the Lord, and that You turn it whichever way You desire. We believe the heart of our President is in Your hand and that You direct his decisions. Father, I ask for godly and wise people to be placed in positions of authority so that we may live quiet and peaceable lives. I thank You that we are more than conquerors through Jesus Christ. We are blessed as a nation because the Word of God is growing and multiplying in our land!

1 Timothy 2:1-3
Proverbs 21:1 AMP
Proverbs 2:10-12
Romans 8:37
Acts 12:24

SALVATION FOR OTHERS

Father, Your Word says that Jesus came to save the lost, and that You want all people to be saved and to live with You forever.

I ask You now to send just the right person to (name) to show him that You love him and that he needs salvation.

Your Word also says that You will deliver those that we pray for because You have washed away our sin. So I stand on Your Word and thank You that (name) will listen to Your Word and come out of the devil's trap and make Jesus his Savior.

Each day after you pray this prayer, thank God for this person's salvation. Praise God for the victory and for the right person to give him God's Word.

Luke 19:10
John 3:15,16
Matthew 9:38
Job 22:30 AMP
2 Timothy 2:26

THE CHURCH

Father, I thank You for Your church, (name of church). Please help us to understand what You want us to do, making us wise about spiritual things and living in a way that will please and honor You. Help us to do Your good works and increase in our knowledge of You. Strengthen us with Your power, so that we can be patient in all things with joy and thanksgiving to You.

You have made us able to share all the good things that belong to Your children in Jesus and have bought our forgiveness through His blood. I thank You for the preachers and teachers at (name of church). I pray that the Spirit of the Lord will rest upon them and make them of quick understanding, because You, Lord, have given them power to preach the Gospel. May they overflow with love for others and learn how to show that love more deeply. I will say only good things about Your Body, the Church, and will always pray for and love them, in the name of Jesus!

Colossians 1:9-14
Isaiah 11:2
Isaiah 61:1
Philippians 1:9
1 Corinthians 12:27
Ephesians 4:31,32

PRAYERS OF PRAISE

Let the words of my mouth and the thoughts of my heart be acceptable in Your sight, Lord—my strength and my redeemer.

Psalm 19:14

I come to You, Father, with singing. Everlasting joy shall be upon my head!

Isaiah 51:11

The joy of the Lord is my strength.

Nehemiah 8:10

Because Your lovingkindness is better than life, my lips shall praise You. I will bless You while I live. I will lift up my hands in Your name.

Psalm 63:3,4 AMP

My mouth shall be filled with Your praise and Your honor all day long.

Psalm 71:8 AMP

Let my prayer be set forth as a sweet smell before You, Lord, and the lifting up of my hands as the evening sacrifice. Set a guard, Lord, before my mouth. Keep watch at the door of my lips.

Psalm 141:2,3 AMP

Your Word is a lamp to my feet and a light to my path.

Psalm 119:105

Bless the Lord, O my soul! All that is within me, bless His holy name!

Psalm 103:1

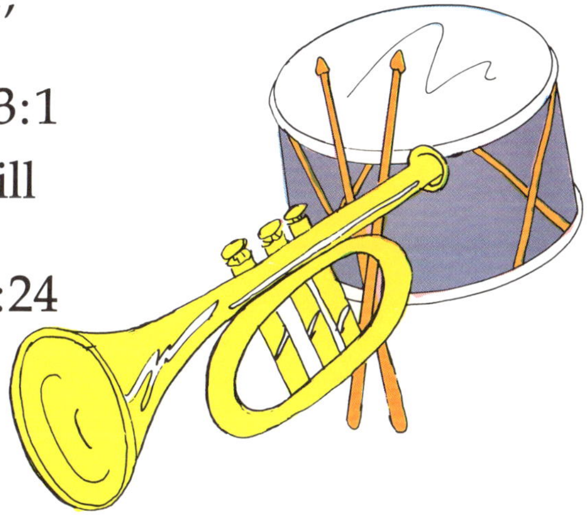

This is the day which the Lord has made; we will rejoice and be glad in it!

Psalm 118:24

Praise the Lord! It is good to sing praises to our God, for He is gracious and lovely. Praise is becoming and appropriate to Him.

Psalm 147:1 AMP

Praise the Lord! Praise God in His sanctuary! Praise Him in the heavens of His power! Praise Him for His mighty acts! Praise Him according to the abundance of His greatness! Praise Him with the trumpet, the lute, and the harp! Praise Him with tambourine and dance; praise Him with stringed and wind instruments or flutes! Praise Him with sounding cymbals; praise Him with loud clashing cymbals! Let everything that has breath and every breath of life praise the Lord! Praise You, Lord! Hallelujah!

Psalm 150 AMP

Little Castle Library

Confessions for Kids
Scriptural Confessions

Prayers That Avail Much For Children
Word-based Prayers

Is Easter Just for Bunnies?
New Life in Christ

God, Are You Really Real?
A Revelation of Jesus

Little Lamb and The Good Shepherd
Psalm 23

The Flight of Orville Wright Caterpillar
An "I Can" Book for Children

Little Faith Builders
Confession Book for ages 4-12

Faith Tales

Little Red Hen
Little Red Ridinghood
The Three Little Pigs
The Three Bears in the Ministry

NEW FROM HARRISON HOUSE

Jack and the Beanstalk
Faith as a Seed
A New Faith Tale
by Beverly Capps Burgess

The Adventure of
Amelia Airheart Butterfly in
Bye, Bye, Dragonfly!
Another "You Can Do It" Book
by Donna Perugini

Available from your local bookstore.

HARRISON HOUSE
P. O. Box 35035 • Tulsa, OK 74153